MATTHEW 26–28

Jesus' Life-Giving Death

A Guided Discovery for Group

Amy Welborn

LOYOLAPRESS.

CHICAGO

LOYOLAPRESS.

3441 N. ASHLAND AVENUE
CHICAGO, ILLINOIS 60657
(800) 621-1008
WWW.LOYOLAPRESS.ORG

Nihil Obstat	Imprimatur
Reverend James P. McIlhone, Ph.D.	Most Reverend Edwin M. Conway, D.D.
Censor Deputatus	Vicar General
October 31, 2003	Archdiocese of Chicago
	November 6, 2003

The *Nihil Obstat* and *Imprimatur* are official declarations that a book is free of doctrinal and moral error. No implication is contained therein that those who have granted the *Nihil Obstat* and *Imprimatur* agree with the content, opinions, or statements expressed.

The Scripture quotations contained herein are from the New Revised Standard Version Bible: Catholic Edition, copyright © 1993 and 1989 by the Division of Christian Education of the National Council of the Churches of Christ in the U.S.A. Used by permission. All rights reserved. Subheadings in Scripture quotations have been added by the author.

The excerpt from Andre Dubus's essay "Bodily Mysteries" (p. 21) is taken from *Meditations from a Movable Chair* (New York: Alfred E. Knopf, 1998), 101–2.

The excerpt from Anthony Bloom (p. 31) is taken from *Beginning to Pray* (New York: Paulist Press, 1970), 20–21.

The excerpt from St. Clare of Assisi (p. 40) is taken from Regis J. Armstrong, trans., ed., *Clare of Assisi: Early Documents* (New York: Paulist Press, 1988), 42.

The excerpt from Francois-Xavier Cardinal Nguyen Van Thuan (p. 41) is taken from *Five Loaves and Two Fish* (Washington, D.C.: Morley Books, 2000), 13–15.

The Greek text of Ignatius of Antioch's letter to Rome (p. 51), with an English translation, may be found in Kirsopp Lake, trans., ed., *The Apostolic Fathers*, vol. 1, Loeb Classical Library (Cambridge, Mass.: Harvard University Press, 1912). Translation by Kevin Perrotta.

The excerpt from *The Little Flowers of St. Francis* (p. 61) is taken from Marion A. Habig, ed., *St. Francis of Assisi* (Chicago: Franciscan Herald Press, 1983), 1448–49.

Excerpts from the English translation of the *Exsultet* (Easter Proclamation) from *The Roman Missal* © 1973, International Committee on English in the Liturgy, Inc. (ICEL). All rights reserved.

The excerpt from St. John Chrysostom (p. 71) can be found at the Web site www.ocf.org/features/EasterSermon.html.

The excerpt from St. Francis de Sales (p. 72) is taken from *Introduction to the Devout Life* (New York: Image Books, 1972), 286.

The excerpt from Richard John Neuhaus (p. 73) is taken from *Death on a Friday Afternoon* (New York: Basic Books, 2000), 226–27.

Interior design by Kay Hartmann/Communique Design
Illustration by Charise Mericle Harper

ISBN 978-0-8294-1990-0
ISBN 0-8294-1990-X

Printed in the United States of America
08 09 10 Bang 10 9 8 7 6 5 4

Contents

How to Use This Guide

You might compare the Bible to a national park. The park is so large that you could spend months, even years, getting to know it. But a brief visit, if carefully planned, can be enjoyable and worthwhile. In a few hours you can drive through the park and pull over at a handful of sites. At each stop you can get out of the car, take a short trail through the woods, listen to the wind blowing in the trees, get a feel for the place.

In this booklet we will drive through a small portion of the Bible, reading six excerpts from the account of the death and resurrection of Jesus presented in the Gospel according to Matthew. Because we will be reading only three chapters from Matthew's Gospel, we will be able to take a leisurely walk through them, thinking carefully about what we are reading and what it means for our lives today. While the section of Matthew we will be looking at is short, it gives us a great deal to reflect on, for in these three chapters Matthew narrates the climactic events in Jesus' life.

This guide provides everything you need to explore the readings from Matthew in six discussions—or to do a six-part exploration on your own. The introduction on page 6 will prepare you to get the most out of your reading. The weekly sections provide explanations that highlight what the Gospel means for us today. Equally important, each section supplies questions that will launch you into fruitful discussion, helping you both to investigate the Gospel for yourself and to learn from one another. If you are using the booklet by yourself, the questions will spur your personal reflection.

Each discussion is meant to be a *guided discovery*.

Guided. None of us is equipped to read the Bible without help. We read the Bible *for* ourselves but not *by* ourselves. Scripture was written to be understood and applied in the community of faith. So each week "A Guide to the Reading," drawing on the work of both modern biblical scholars and Christian writers of the past, supplies background and explanations. The guide will help you grasp Matthew's message. Think of it as a friendly park ranger who points out noteworthy details and explains what you're looking at so you can appreciate things for yourself.

Discovery. The purpose is for *you* to interact with Matthew's account of Jesus' death and resurrection. "Questions for Careful Reading" is a tool to help you dig into the text and examine it carefully. "Questions for Application" will help you consider what these words mean for your life here and now. Each week concludes with an "Approach to Prayer" section that helps you respond to God's word. Supplementary "Living Tradition" and "Saints in the Making" sections offer the thoughts and experiences of Christians past and present. By showing what the Gospel has meant to others, these sections will help you consider what it means for you.

How long are the discussion sessions? We've assumed you will have about an hour and a half when you get together. If you have less time, you'll find that most of the elements can be shortened somewhat.

Is homework necessary? You will get the most out of your discussions if you read the weekly material and prepare your answers to the questions in advance of each meeting. If participants are not able to prepare, have someone read the "Guide to the Reading" sections aloud at the points where they appear.

What about leadership? If you happen to have a world-class biblical scholar in your group, by all means ask him or her to lead the discussions. In the absence of any professional Scripture scholars, or even accomplished amateur biblical scholars, you can still have a first-class Bible discussion. Choose two or three people to take turns as facilitators, and have everyone read "Suggestions for Bible Discussion Groups" (page 76) before beginning.

Does everyone need a guide? a Bible? Everyone in the group will need their own copy of this booklet. It contains the text of the portions of the Gospel that are discussed, so a Bible is not absolutely necessary—but each participant will find it useful to have one. You should have at least one Bible on hand for your discussions. (See page 80 for recommendations.)

How do we get started? Before you begin, take a look at the suggestions for Bible discussion groups (page 76) or individuals (page 79).

The Mystery of Jesus' Suffering

Few stories are more familiar to us as Christians than the Gospel accounts of the passion, death, and resurrection of Jesus of Nazareth. All four Gospels tell essentially the same tale. After an inspiring and tumultuous public ministry, Jesus and his disciples went to Jerusalem at the time of the Passover feast. After celebrating a special last meal with his closest followers, Jesus was arrested in an olive grove just outside the city walls. His fearful disciples deserted him. After interrogating Jesus, the religious and civil authorities collaborated to do away with him. He was flogged, then executed by crucifixion, and buried. Some days later (on the third day, by ancient reckoning) his followers saw him again—alive.

From these events the Christian faith was born. From earliest times, Christians have believed that through the suffering and death of Jesus, God has brought the greatest good that humanity could hope for: victory over sin and death. Yet for all its familiarity, the story of the suffering, death, and resurrection of Jesus is also a great mystery. These events shocked Jesus' followers at the time, and by all indications, they continued to puzzle and confuse the members of the infant Christian Church that was born in the outpouring of the Holy Spirit at Pentecost. The four Gospels were written to explain the significance of Jesus to these early Christians, especially to answer questions about Jesus' last days. Why did he die? What did it mean that he rose from the dead? How do these facts change the way we live now and how we view the future?

These are questions we ask ourselves today. We may be the heirs to two thousand years of theological reflection on the meaning of Jesus' suffering, death, and resurrection, but we hardly know everything there is to know about them. They are historical facts, but their meaning is infinitely rich and inexhaustible. The Gospel accounts of the Passion (a traditional word for Jesus' suffering and death) were written for people very different from us in culture, language, and religious background. But we need to understand the meaning of Jesus' passion and resurrection just as they did. These accounts are written for us, too.

In this book, we will examine the portrayal of the passion and resurrection of Jesus in chapters 26–28 of Matthew's Gospel. We will take special pains to explore the meaning of these texts in our lives today. Matthew describes the central work of Jesus in coming to live among us. His account, as much as any text in Scripture, has the potential to change the way we live our lives.

Matthew and his audience. An ancient tradition links the Gospel we will be reading with Matthew, one of Jesus' twelve apostles (Matthew 9:9—Scripture citations in this book refer to the Gospel of Matthew except where noted). But most scholars today think that Matthew's Gospel is the work of a later author who drew on oral and written traditions coming from Jesus' first followers. Most scholars think that Matthew, whoever he was, probably completed his Gospel between the years AD 70 and 90.

Matthew seems to have written his Gospel for a mostly Jewish Christian community. We can deduce this from the attention he devotes to showing how Jesus fulfilled prophecies in the Scriptures of the Jewish people (the writings that Christians call the Old Testament).

At the same time, Matthew's readers seem to have been seeking to evangelize gentiles. An indication of this is Matthew's emphasis on gentiles who recognize Jesus' identity. At the cross, a Roman military officer, a centurion, is among those who first acknowledge Jesus to be the Son of God. Another gentile—Herod's wife—receives special insight into Jesus through a dream. At the very end of the Gospel, Jesus specifically directs his disciples to bring the good news of God's kingdom not just to the people of Israel but to the entire world.

Matthew's Gospel was written to explain Jesus to these audiences. Like the other three Gospels, it is not a history in the modern sense. It is rooted in history, in the testimony of eye-witnesses, but it is not intended to simply recount these events. Rather, Matthew wrote in such a way as to reveal the *meaning* of the events. He wrote to help us perceive who Jesus truly is and what he has done for us—and to help us respond to him.

The setting. The events in Matthew's Passion narrative take place in and around Jerusalem. At the time the city may have had some 50,000 to 100,000 inhabitants. Jesus arrives in Jerusalem via Bethany, a town about two miles east of Jerusalem. The following events take place at sites that are within a mere square mile or so.

The events of Jesus' passion took place around the year AD 30 against the backdrop of the Jewish Feast of Passover. The Gospel writers saw it as no accident that Jesus celebrated his final meal and met his death in the midst of this celebration of God's liberation of the Israelites.

The roots of the Feast of Passover—or as it was known in the time of Jesus, the Feast of Unleavened Bread (26:17)—are found in the Old Testament book of Exodus (see especially chapter 12). The feast celebrates the Israelites' release from Egyptian bondage by the miraculous power of God. God called Moses to lead the Israelites to freedom, which was accomplished after a series of plagues convinced Egypt's king to let the Israelites go. The final plague, the death of the firstborn sons of Egypt, took place on the night before the Israelites were allowed to leave Egypt. On that night, the Israelites put the blood of a lamb on the lintels and doorposts of their homes so that the angel of death would pass over their homes, leaving their own firstborn alive. Meanwhile they ate a supper that featured unleavened bread, which, not needing time to rise, was suited for their hasty preparations to depart.

In the centuries that followed, the Jewish people remembered that night by celebrating the Passover festival. At the Passover meal, on the first night of the seven-day festival, they retold the story of their redemption by God's mighty hand and reaffirmed their participation in that redemption. On the after-noon before the feast began, a lamb or goat was taken to be slaughtered at the temple. That evening, as the celebration began, groups of families and friends gathered to eat meat, unleavened bread, and bitter herbs, and to drink a series of cups of wine accompanied by blessings.

Jesus made this Passover meal his last meal with his disciples. As they ate, he used the Passover meal to explain the meaning of his death as a sacrifice that would liberate people from sin and form a new bond, or covenant, between God and human beings. He established the meal as a celebration of this new sacrifice and new covenant. By continuing to eat this meal after his death and resurrection, his disciples would experience God's power liberating them from the bondage of sin and death and would be renewed in this new covenant. Every time we share Eucharist— the reenactment of this Last Supper and of Jesus' death—we eat Jesus' body and blood and receive God's forgiving, healing, and life-giving love given through Jesus' death and resurrection.

The cast of characters. The primary characters in Matthew's narrative of the Passion are Jesus and his apostles. During his ministry, Jesus called disciples to follow him, choosing twelve in particular (called apostles—"those who are sent") to receive his teaching at close hand and to continue his ministry after his death. Matthew tells us that the apostles responded immediately to Jesus' call, but that the journey from that point was not a straight one. The apostles quite often did not understand Jesus' teachings. They seemed to be particularly resistant to his constant instruction that being his disciples involves suffering, and that his own life would end at the hands of others.

So, while the apostles have faithfully followed Jesus through his ministry, right up to time he enters Jerusalem, they have not completely understood his words and actions. The result of this failure to understand becomes evident in our readings. As Jesus enters his passion, the disciples falter and turn away from him, giving us much to reflect on regarding our own discipleship to Jesus.

Besides Jesus and the apostles, Jewish and Roman leaders populate Matthew's account of the Passion. Caiaphas was the high priest in the temple in Jerusalem, the religious center of Judaism. He held office from about AD 18 to 36. The high priest was the head of the Sanhedrin, the council that governed the temple in Jerusalem under Roman authority. This body of elders could function as a court, but many scholars believe it was restricted from imposing the death penalty. The Sanhedrin was an important authority in Jerusalem, but it did not reflect the views of all Jews, or even of all residents of Jerusalem. The members of the Sanhedrin had their own agenda, which involved, in part, their interest in continuing their profitable relationship with the Roman regime. This factored into their decision to arrest Jesus and seek his execution (see page 74).

Pontius Pilate, the Roman governor, or more precisely the prefect of the region, was appointed in AD 26. As the highest local representative of the Roman regime, he exercised the power of life and death over the inhabitants. Pilate often clashed with his Jewish subjects. He brought offensive images of the emperor into Jerusalem and took money from the temple treasury to pay for an aqueduct. He is remembered as insensitive and cruel, although ancient historians report that when threatened with unrest, he might back off from a decision.

Who is Jesus? Matthew's Gospel was intended to solve the problem of confusion and misunderstanding about Jesus' identity and mission. At the time, not even the disciples, who were closest to him, understood who he was and what he came to accomplish. The masses of Jewish people were no more enlightened. In Jesus' time, there were widespread expectations among the Jewish people that at some point in the future God would send a messiah, a saving king, to release the Israelites from their subjugation by Rome. They expected a messiah who would have a political, as well as a religious, role. But Jesus did not involve himself in political life. He spoke of a kingdom, and while it concerned life in this world, it was not a national kingdom defined by geographical boundaries with political institutions.

Matthew presents Jesus as the Messiah who exceeded all expectations. He is a savior in a wider, deeper, more spiritual sense than expected. He is the Son of God. Through him, God's reconciliation and healing have come among men and women—and not just for Israel, but for the entire world. Jesus is, indeed, "Emmanuel," or "God is with us" (1:23).

Yet Jesus does truly fulfill God's promises to the people of Israel. Despite the unexpectedness of his ministry and his death, Jesus is the culminating point for God's saving action, which God began long before, at the time of the Exodus, and earlier with Abraham. In order to make this point, Matthew rarely misses an opportunity to draw our attention to how an event in Jesus' life was prophesied hundreds of years before. He does this, however, not only to show that Jesus *is* the Messiah but also to help us understand what *kind* of Messiah he is.

In this book we will examine two important examples of Matthew's use of the Old Testament: Mathew's references to Isaiah 52–53 and to Psalm 22.

Chapters 40–55 of Isaiah were probably written during the sixth century before Christ, when many of the people of Israel, defeated in war, were living in exile in Babylonia (present-day Iraq). Within these chapters are found descriptions of a "servant" of God who suffers greatly and through whose suffering, reconciliation comes to Israel. In the centuries before Jesus, Jewish people did not connect this suffering figure with the expected messiah. But Matthew draws attention to it and squarely identifies Jesus as this "suffering servant."

Matthew accomplishes something similar by quoting the verses of Psalm 22 that Jesus prayed while dying on the cross. Psalm 22 is a prayer offered to God by a person in great pain. This prayer describes cruel suffering at the hands of tormenters and apparent abandonment by God. In spite of this, the prayer also expresses strong trust in God and his power to save.

These passages from Isaiah and Psalms suggest that suffering is not necessarily a sign of God's displeasure and that, indeed, God can bring great good out of suffering. These passages helped Matthew's community understand the role of Jesus' suffering in God's plan and were an important lens through which Matthew viewed Jesus' suffering.

This lens is as helpful for modern readers as it was for those who pondered Jesus' death two thousand years ago. The sight of Jesus suffering on the cross can still confuse and puzzle us. We, too, have trouble seeing how God can use suffering for his purposes. The questions that Matthew seeks to answer are questions not only of the first century but of the twenty-first century as well.

The Time Draws Near

Questions to Begin

15 minutes
Use a question or two to get warmed up for the reading.

1 What celebration would you be willing to spend a lot of time and money on?

2 What do you do when an awkward moment occurs at a social gathering?
❏ I quietly pray that the moment will pass.
❏ I create a distraction by spilling my drink.
❏ I quickly change the subject.
❏ I try to help smooth out tensions.
❏ I head for the door.

5 minutes
Read the passage aloud. Let individuals take turns reading paragraphs.

The Reading: Matthew 26:1–35

The Son of Man Will Be Handed Over

1 When Jesus had finished saying all these things, he said to his disciples, 2 "You know that after two days the Passover is coming, and the Son of Man will be handed over to be crucified."

3 Then the chief priests and the elders of the people gathered in the palace of the high priest, who was called Caiaphas, 4 and they conspired to arrest Jesus by stealth and kill him. 5 But they said, "Not during the festival, or there may be a riot among the people."

Why This Waste?

6 Now while Jesus was at Bethany in the house of Simon the leper, 7 a woman came to him with an alabaster jar of very costly ointment, and she poured it on his head as he sat at the table. 8 But when the disciples saw it, they were angry and said, "Why this waste? 9 For this ointment could have been sold for a large sum, and the money given to the poor." 10 But Jesus, aware of this, said to them, "Why do you trouble the woman? She has performed a good service for me. 11 For you always have the poor with you, but you will not always have me. 12 By pouring this ointment on my body she has prepared me for burial. 13 Truly I tell you, wherever this good news is proclaimed in the whole world, what she has done will be told in remembrance of her."

What Will You Give Me?

14 Then one of the twelve, who was called Judas Iscariot, went to the chief priests 15 and said, "What will you give me if I betray him to you?" They paid him thirty pieces of silver. 16 And from that moment he began to look for an opportunity to betray him.

Surely Not I?

17 On the first day of Unleavened Bread the disciples came to Jesus, saying, "Where do you want us to make the preparations for you to eat the Passover?" 18 He said, "Go into the city to a certain man, and say to him, 'The Teacher says, My time is near; I will keep the

Passover at your house with my disciples.'" 19 So the disciples did as Jesus had directed them, and they prepared the Passover meal.

20 When it was evening, he took his place with the twelve; 21 and while they were eating, he said, "Truly I tell you, one of you will betray me." 22 And they became greatly distressed and began to say to him one after another, "Surely not I, Lord?" 23 He answered, "The one who has dipped his hand into the bowl with me will betray me. 24 The Son of Man goes as it is written of him, but woe to that one by whom the Son of Man is betrayed! It would have been better for that one not to have been born." 25 Judas, who betrayed him, said, "Surely not I, Rabbi?" He replied, "You have said so."

Take, Eat

26 While they were eating, Jesus took a loaf of bread, and after blessing it he broke it, gave it to the disciples, and said, "Take, eat; this is my body." 27 Then he took a cup, and after giving thanks he gave it to them, saying, "Drink from it, all of you; 28 for this is my blood of the covenant, which is poured out for many for the forgiveness of sins. 29 I tell you, I will never again drink of this fruit of the vine until that day when I drink it new with you in my Father's kingdom."

30 When they had sung the hymn, they went out to the Mount of Olives.

You Will Deny Me

31 Then Jesus said to them, "You will all become deserters because of me this night; for it is written,

'I will strike the shepherd,
    and the sheep of the flock will be scattered.'
32 But after I am raised up, I will go ahead of you to Galilee." 33 Peter said to him, "Though all become deserters because of you, I will never desert you." 34 Jesus said to him, "Truly I tell you, this very night, before the cock crows, you will deny me three times." 35 Peter said to him, "Even though I must die with you, I will not deny you." And so said all the disciples.

Questions for Careful Reading

10 minutes
Choose questions according to your interest and time.

1 Reread 26:5. Why might the arrest of Jesus trigger a riot? Why would the religious leaders want to avoid that possibility?

2 Reread the remarks by Jesus' disciples and by Jesus himself regarding the woman's use of expensive oil to anoint him (26:8–13). Why do Jesus and his disciples evaluate the woman's action differently?

3 How well does Jesus know his disciples? Cite particular statements by Jesus. How do you think the disciples felt about his knowledge of them?

4 Does this passage leave you with an impression of Jesus as a victim of events? Why or why not?

A Guide to the Reading

If participants have not read this section already, read it aloud. Otherwise go on to "Questions for Application."

26:1–35. Two things are clear: Jesus is keenly aware of the horrible events that are about to unfold, and these events are connected to God's interaction with the people of Israel in the past. Jesus predicts that he will be betrayed at Passover (26:2), thus indicating that what will happen will be no surprise to him and that, in some mysterious way, the unfolding events will be a continuation of what God did for his people when he brought them out of slavery in Egypt and made a covenant with them in the Sinai desert.

The religious leaders at first seem determined to avoid arresting Jesus during the Passover feast, when Jerusalem is bustling with pilgrims. Many in the festival crowds would be hoping that Jesus was the liberating Messiah. Their feeling of anticipation of liberation from the Romans might especially be raised by the Passover celebration, which brings a reminder of God's liberation of their ancestors from Egypt. In this situation, arresting Jesus might spark public disturbances—disturbances that the Roman authorities expected the temple authorities to curb, or they would.

A tragic paradox emerges: The religious leaders are plotting to arrest the one who has come as the messiah to bring freedom from the bondage of sin and death. They will end up arresting him during the very feast that celebrates their people's freedom from bondage.

At a dinner in a home in Bethany, a village on the outskirts of Jerusalem, a woman anoints Jesus with perfumed oil. Anointing was an expression of honor; it was also an action associated with burial in Jewish tradition. While the disciples fret about the cost of the oil, Jesus confronts them with the hard reality of his approaching death. He has told them again and again of the suffering that awaits him in Jerusalem (16:21; 17:22–23; 20:18–19), yet they still do not seem to understand. Does this woman sense what the male disciples do not—that Jesus' death is imminent?

The religious leaders decide to abandon their plan to leave Jesus alone during the Passover when suddenly the apostle Judas appears, offering to facilitate Jesus' arrest. The thirty pieces of silver may sound like a hefty sum, but Matthew's readers would have known that it is not. In fact, it is an insulting valuation. In

Exodus 21:32, the owner of an ox who had gored a slave is instructed to pay this amount in compensation to the slave's owner.

Meanwhile, Jesus calmly proceeds with his plans for the Passover. The disciples are sent into Jerusalem to carry out arrangements that Jesus has previously made. Their preparations during the afternoon would have included procuring a lamb or kid, taking it to the temple for slaughter, and ensuring that the home for the feast was cleared of all leaven.

The Passover meal was and is a celebration of God's saving action. Those who eat the meal remember that God miraculously rescued the people of Israel from slavery in Egypt. The menu and the prayers during the meal are reminders of Israel's identity as God's people. The remembering is more than simply bringing the Exodus to mind. The participants in the meal remind themselves that they, too, are the recipients of God's deliverance, just as much as the original Exodus generation. Throughout the meal the participants recall that they belong to the same people that God rescued from slavery in Egypt. They note that God continues to be present with them, as he was with their ancestors. Every Passover meal gathers the new generation into the divine presence and renews their expectation that God will fulfill anew his promise of freedom.

Jesus takes this traditional meal and invests it with new meaning. He blesses the bread and wine and tells the apostles to partake of these as his own body and blood. This must have been puzzling, even shocking, for the disciples. Jews are forbidden to eat meat that has blood in it, and the idea of eating human flesh would have seemed as strange to them as it does to us. But in this way, Jesus lets the disciples know that his death, which is imminent, will be a means of deliverance—a sacrifice "for the forgiveness of sins" (26:28). And he shows them that they will share in that deliverance from sin and death and will experience a new covenant—a deeper, more intimate relationship—with God.

Twice during the meal Jesus predicts betrayal. The apostles protest that they could never betray Jesus. As we will see, their strong convictions will soon fail.

Questions for Application

40 minutes
Choose questions according to your interest and time.

1 The disciples' complaints in Bethany that anointing Jesus was a waste of resources points to tensions about how we should spend our time and money. Should we devote time to prayer or to serving others? What do you think?

2 Jesus shows that he knows his disciples better than they know themselves. When have you become aware of Jesus' knowledge of your life? How have you responded?

3 Jesus was betrayed by a friend. Have you experienced betrayal? Are forgiveness and reconciliation possible after a betrayal? How?

4 Jesus ate the Passover meal at the home of someone who knew him (26:18). Think of Jesus eating in your home with you and those with whom you live. How might your awareness of Jesus' presence with you as you eat together affect how you relate to each other at the table?

5 How has your appreciation of the Eucharist grown over time? How might reading Matthew's account of the Last Supper increase your appreciation of the Eucharist?

6 How well do you think Jesus' disciples understood what he was doing at the Last Supper? What helped them afterward to grow in understanding? What has helped you understand the Eucharist? How could you continue to grow in understanding of what Jesus does in the Eucharist?

7 For personal reflection: Jesus shares himself with his disciples at the Last Supper even though he is acutely aware of their weaknesses. What light does this cast on Jesus' relationship with you? on how you might approach him in the Sacrament?

You should also be prepared to share your own personal stories that are related to the discussion questions.

Stephen Arterburn, The Every Man Series Bible Studies

Approach to Prayer

15 minutes
Use this approach—or create your own!

◆ Reread 26:26–30 aloud. Take a few moments for silent reflection. The hymn that Jesus and the apostles sang before walking to the Mount of Olives (26:30) probably included Psalms 114–118, which are traditionally sung after the Passover meal. Pray Psalm 118 together. If everyone has the same translation, you may pray it all together or divide into two groups and read successive verses alternately. If participants have different translations, ask one participant to read the psalm aloud for the group.

Saints in the Making

No Longer Alone

This section is a supplement for individual reading.

Andre Dubus (1936–1999) was an American fiction writer and essayist. Born in Louisiana, he spent time in the Marines before he settled down to a life of writing and teaching. Known for evocative, deeply spiritual, yet sometimes ambiguous stories, Dubus's life changed dramatically one night in 1986 when he stopped his car on a highway to help two motorists in distress. As they were standing by the road, another car approached at high speed and struck the group, killing one of the motorists and causing such damage to Dubus that he was confined to a wheelchair for the rest of his life.

In his many essays, collected in *Broken Vessels* and *Meditations from a Movable Chair,* Dubus reflected on life, limitations, death, and his Catholic faith. In "Bodily Mysteries," he pondered Jesus' gift of himself at the Last Supper and in every celebration of Eucharist since, as he recalls attending Mass.

I am writing this on a Wednesday. The past five days have been bad ones, and I have prayed in desperation, prayed for strength, hope, love, gratitude. This morning I resumed my physical contact with God: I went to Mass and received the Eucharist. . . .

This morning, after struggling with two doors to get into the church, I settled in my chair and watched the priest lifting the unleavened bread, and saying, "This is my body," lifting the chalice of wine, saying, "This is my blood of the new covenant" . . . and peace of mind came to me and, yes, happiness too, for I was no longer a broken body, alone in my chair. I was me, all of me, in wholeness of spirit. The old man assisting the priest handed me the Host, and I placed it in my mouth and was in harmony with the old man, the priest, the walking communicants passing me and my chair to receive the Eucharist; one with all people in pain and joy and passion, one with the physical universe, with Christ, with the timeless dimension of the spirit, which has no past or future but only now; one with God. Me: flawed and foolish me. I drove my car to church and consumed God.

YOUR WILL BE DONE

Questions to Begin

15 minutes
Use a question or two to get warmed up for the reading.

1 What's your strategy for not falling asleep when you're tired but have to stay awake?

2 When have you slept through something important?

5 minutes
Read the passage aloud. Let individuals take turns reading
paragraphs.

The Reading: Matthew 26:36–56

Stay Awake with Me

36 Then Jesus went with them to a place called Gethsemane; and he said to his disciples, "Sit here while I go over there and pray." 37 He took with him Peter and the two sons of Zebedee, and began to be grieved and agitated. 38 Then he said to them, "I am deeply grieved, even to death; remain here, and stay awake with me." 39 And going a little farther, he threw himself on the ground and prayed, "My Father, if it is possible, let this cup pass from me; yet not what I want but what you want."

40 Then he came to the disciples and found them sleeping; and he said to Peter, "So, could you not stay awake with me one hour? 41 Stay awake and pray that you may not come into the time of trial; the spirit indeed is willing, but the flesh is weak."

42 Again he went away for the second time and prayed, "My Father, if this cannot pass unless I drink it, your will be done." 43 Again he came and found them sleeping, for their eyes were heavy. 44 So leaving them again, he went away and prayed for the third time, saying the same words. 45 Then he came to the disciples and said to them, "Are you still sleeping and taking your rest? See, the hour is at hand, and the Son of Man is betrayed into the hands of sinners. 46 Get up, let us be going. See, my betrayer is at hand."

Put Your Sword Away

47 While he was still speaking, Judas, one of the twelve, arrived; with him was a large crowd with swords and clubs, from the chief priests and the elders of the people. 48 Now the betrayer had given them a sign, saying, "The one I will kiss is the man; arrest him." 49 At once he came up to Jesus and said, "Greetings, Rabbi!" and kissed him. 50 Jesus said to him, "Friend, do what you are here to do." Then they came and laid hands on Jesus and arrested him. 51 Suddenly, one of those with Jesus put his hand on his sword, drew it, and struck the slave of the high priest, cutting off his ear. 52 Then Jesus said to him, "Put your sword back into its place; for all who take the sword will perish by the sword. 53 Do you think that I cannot appeal to my Father, and he will at once send me more

than twelve legions of angels? 54 But how then would the scriptures be fulfilled, which say it must happen in this way?" 55 At that hour Jesus said to the crowds, "Have you come out with swords and clubs to arrest me as though I were a bandit? Day after day I sat in the temple teaching, and you did not arrest me. 56 But all this has taken place, so that the scriptures of the prophets may be fulfilled." Then all the disciples deserted him and fled.

Questions for Careful Reading

10 minutes
Choose questions according to your interest and time.

1 How does Jesus' prayer in 26:39, 42 echo his earlier words to the disciples and crowd in 6:9–13?

2 How would you express in your own words Jesus' explanation for why he submits to arrest (26:54)? Does anything in last week's reading (26:1–35) shed further light on why Jesus allows himself to be captured?

3 How does the behavior of Jesus' disciples at the beginning and the end of this passage compare with the words of Peter, the lead disciple, in 26:33?

4 What qualities of character does Jesus show in the first episode of this reading (26:36–46)? What qualities does he show in the second episode (26:47–56)?

5 Jesus says that "all who take the sword will perish by the sword" (26:52). What does Jesus mean by this?

A Guide to the Reading

If participants have not read this section already, read it aloud. Otherwise go on to "Questions for Application."

26:36–56. The Passover meal completed, Jesus and his disciples walk out through an eastern gate in the Jerusalem city wall and cross the Kidron valley to the Mount of Olives. There they stop, perhaps in the company of other pilgrims camped for the night, in a garden called Gethsemane, which means "oil press."

Jesus takes Peter, James, and John to a spot away from the other disciples. These were three of the first disciples called by Jesus, and they alone were chosen to witness his transfiguration on a mountain, when he displayed his heavenly splendor to them (17:1–13). Now he asks them to watch with him as he prepares for his suffering.

But they don't. Jesus prays three times, in obvious struggle. After each prayer he returns to his three friends and finds them asleep. The physical distance between Jesus and the three apostles seems to reflect an emotional and spiritual distance. The contrast between his wakefulness and their slumber marks a difference in readiness for what lies ahead. Because the disciples sleep, they are unprepared and weak when Jesus' "hour" comes (26:45). "The hour" is an expression meaning "a decisive moment." Here it refers to the moment when God's plan for the human race will be accomplished through Jesus' death and resurrection.

Jesus had told the disciples of the importance of being prepared for the unexpected timing of God's actions. "Keep awake!" he had said, urgently reminding them not to be like a man who was robbed because he slept (24:42–43; compare 25:13). Despite Jesus' repeated warnings to be awake and alert, the apostles drift off to sleep.

The consequences of Jesus' and his followers' different use of the minutes in the orchard of Gethsemane soon become obvious. Jesus, who has submitted to the Father's will through his prayer, is strengthened to meet suffering. The disciples, not having submitted themselves to God's will in prayer, are unprepared to meet the crisis with courage and loyalty. When Jesus is arrested, all the disciples panic and flee (26:56).

Matthew's portrayal of Jesus illuminates both his divine and human dimensions. With divine insight Jesus alone knows the course that events are to take; he sees into his followers' hearts.

Yet, as any man facing death, he struggles to accept the Father's will. With a human dread of pain, he asks if there might be another way to achieve the Father's saving purpose.

When the hour arrives, it is announced by the most tragically ironic gesture in all of Scripture—the kiss of Judas. Once again (compare 26:25), Judas addresses Jesus as "Rabbi," that is, "teacher"—a title used in Matthew's account by those who have only a restricted recognition of who Jesus is. Jesus, in turn, calls Judas "friend," a term of intimacy that here serves to underline the immense gulf that has now opened up between him and Judas (20:13; 22:12). Jesus offered Judas a friendship beyond any human valuation, but Judas has rejected it.

Judas' kiss is a prearranged sign to enable the temple officials to identify Jesus among the crowd in the dark olive grove. As often happens in tense confrontations, someone panics and resorts to violence (26:51). Jesus responds by warning, as he had before (5:39), that violence is futile. Jesus displays a confidence in God's ultimate protection. He asserts that he certainly could be protected by God from physical harm but has chosen not to be. He is confident that his submission to the Father's plan will take him, on the other side of suffering, to something even greater than rescue from his present danger.

Jesus has had ample opportunity to escape the arrest that he knew was being plotted. Throughout the evening, he could have simply returned to Bethany, leaving his enemies behind him in Jerusalem. Jesus' temptation in Gethsemane to avoid the suffering that loomed before him at the end of his ministry echoed an earlier bout of temptation at the beginning of his public life. Then the devil tempted Jesus to use angels for protection (4:6). Here, Jesus acknowledges those same angels' presence and power (26:53). In the earlier incident, Jesus had turned away from the temptation and had embraced God's word. Through his prayer in Gethsemane he has been strengthened to do the same.

Matthew makes it clear that Jesus was not a helpless victim. Death was a possibility to which he assented, a dreadful imposition to which he chose to submit, in accord with God's mysterious purpose for the world.

Questions for Application

40 minutes
Choose questions according to your interest and time.

1 Jesus asked his disciples to watch with him in the garden as he faced his suffering. What challenges are involved in being present with a friend who is suffering? Have you ever been reluctant to help a friend who was suffering? What have you learned about effective and ineffective ways of being with someone who is suffering?

2 When you are suffering, what words and actions by others do you find most helpful and comforting? What is not helpful?

3 What would you have said to Jesus in the garden if you were a disciple who stayed with him?

4 In Gethsemane, Jesus faced the temptation to flee from God's plan for him. What helps you move ahead with something you feel God wants you to do, even when it is difficult?

5 When Jesus was arrested, the disciples acted poorly because they were confused and frightened. What helps you to stay grounded during frightening situations?

6 Jesus' rebuke to Peter (26:52) implies that violence begets violence. How widely can this principle be applied? Are there limits to its application?

7 Peter was sure that he would remain faithful to Jesus, but he did not foresee his own weakness. How could he have foreseen and compensated for his weakness? How much can a person foresee and compensate for their weaknesses?

You model openness. You set the pace. Honesty breeds honesty in a discussion.

Stephen Arterburn, The Every Man Series Bible Studies

Approach to Prayer

15 minutes
Use this approach—or create your own!

◆ Have a member of the group read 26:36–39 aloud, slowly. Invite participants to reflect silently on situations in their lives where they are struggling to discern or accept God's will. End by slowly praying the Our Father aloud together.

Saints in the Making

Her Own Gethsemane

This section is a supplement for individual reading.

At Gethsemane, Jesus struggled with God's will as he contemplated the suffering that lay ahead of him and waited for the men to come who were going to put him to death. At any moment, he could have fled. But he stayed and accepted his death out of love for those he had come to save—us.

In his book *Beginning to Pray*, Russian Orthodox Archbishop Anthony Bloom (1914–2003) tells the story of a young woman who experienced her own Gethsemane. It happened sometime between 1917 and 1920, during the Communist revolution in Russia. The country was torn by civil war. A young woman with two children, whose husband was fighting for the czar, lived in a village that fell under the control of the Red Army. She hid, knowing that her life was in terrible danger.

One evening, a young woman from the neighborhood, whom she did not know, came to the door and told her that her hiding place had been discovered and her arrest was imminent. The mother must flee with her children. This young woman, named Natalie, would take her place and claim her identity when the Communists came. "But you will be shot," the mother said. "Yes, but I have no children," Natalie replied, and she stayed behind.

We can imagine what happened then. We can see the night coming, wrapping in darkness, in gloom, in cold and damp, this cottage. We can see there a woman who was waiting for her death to come and we can remember the Garden of Gethsemane. We can imagine Natalie asking that this cup should pass her by and being met like Christ by divine silence. We can imagine her turning in intention towards those who might have supported her, but who were out of reach. The disciples of Christ slept; and she could turn to no one without betraying. We can imagine that more than once she prayed that at least her sacrifice should not be in vain. . . .

Probably she thought more than once that in one minute she could be secure! It was enough to open the door and the moment she was in the street she no longer was that woman, she became herself again. It was enough to deny her false, her shared identity. But she died, shot. The mother and the children escaped.

PARALLEL TRIALS

Questions to Begin

15 minutes
Use a question or two to get warmed up for the reading.

---

1 How do you cope when you feel put on the spot with a difficult question?
☐ I fumble around for words.
☐ I blurt out the first thing that comes into my head.
☐ I'm pretty good at thinking on my feet.
☐ I like unexpected challenges.

---

2 If you wanted to disguise your identity, how would you change your appearance?

---

3 When you want to escape from pressures for a while, where do you go?

5 minutes
Read the passage aloud. Let individuals take turns reading
paragraphs.

The Reading: Matthew 26:57–75

You Say So

57 Those who had arrested Jesus took him to Caiaphas the high priest, in whose house the scribes and the elders had gathered. 58 But Peter was following him at a distance, as far as the courtyard of the high priest; and going inside, he sat with the guards in order to see how this would end.
     59 Now the chief priests and the whole council were looking for false testimony against Jesus so that they might put him to death, 60 but they found none, though many false witnesses came forward. At last two came forward 61 and said, "This fellow said, 'I am able to destroy the temple of God and to build it in three days.'" 62 The high priest stood up and said, "Have you no answer? What is it that they testify against you?" 63 But Jesus was silent. Then the high priest said to him, "I put you under oath before the living God, tell us if you are the Messiah, the Son of God." 64 Jesus said to him, "You have said so. But I tell you,
          From now on you will see the Son of Man
               seated at the right hand of Power
               and coming on the clouds of heaven."
65 Then the high priest tore his clothes and said, "He has blasphemed! Why do we still need witnesses? You have now heard his blasphemy. 66 What is your verdict?" They answered, "He deserves death."
     67 Then they spat in his face and struck him; and some slapped him, 68 saying, "Prophesy to us, you Messiah! Who is it that struck you?"

I Do Not Know Him

69 Now Peter was sitting outside in the courtyard. A servant-girl came to him and said, "You also were with Jesus the Galilean." 70 But he denied it before all of them, saying, "I do not know what you are talking about." 71 When he went out to the porch, another servant-girl saw him, and she said to the bystanders, "This man was with Jesus of Nazareth." 72 Again he denied it with an oath, "I do not know the man." 73 After a little while the bystanders came up

and said to Peter, "Certainly you are also one of them, for your accent betrays you." 74 Then he began to curse, and he swore an oath, "I do not know the man!" At that moment the cock crowed. 75 Then Peter remembered what Jesus had said: "Before the cock crows, you will deny me three times." And he went out and wept bitterly.

10 minutes
Choose questions according to your interest and time.

1 What kind of testimony against Jesus might the religious leaders have been looking for?

2 What does the testimony offered against Jesus indicate about him?

3 In what way is Jesus' statement in 26:64 an answer to Caiaphas's question?

4 While Jesus is mocked as a false prophet (26:67–68), Peter is responding to bystanders' assertions that he is a follower of Jesus (26:69–74). What do Peter's answers indicate about whether Jesus is a false prophet? (Look back to 26:34.)

5 Does the interrogation before the high priest actually uncover any wrongdoing by Jesus?

A Guide to the Reading

If participants have not read this section already, read it aloud. Otherwise go on to "Questions for Application."

26:57–75. The temple authorities have already decided to put Jesus to death (26:3–4). Their task, after arresting him, is to make a case against him that will warrant the death penalty under both Jewish and Roman law. In this reading they are searching for a religious warrant for his execution. In next week's reading, they formulate an accusation that will bring his condemnation under Roman law.

The religious warrant they find is blasphemy, or insulting God by claiming to share his status or power. Under the Mosaic Law, those found guilty of blasphemy were executed by stoning (Leviticus 24:16). Jesus had already incurred the religious authorities' suspicion of blasphemy by asserting that people's eternal destiny depended on how they responded to him and his proclamation of God's kingdom (5:11–12; 7:24–27; 10:32–33). He declared people's sins forgiven, a role that belonged to God, prompting witnesses to say, "This man is blaspheming" (9:3).

In the impromptu hearing after Jesus' arrest, the authorities have trouble locating witnesses who can give clear, specific testimony against Jesus. The council does find two witnesses (the minimum needed according to the Mosaic Law) who accuse Jesus of saying something about the temple that indicated that he shares in God's power.

Jesus refuses to answer these charges. Matthew may intend Jesus' silence to remind us of the silently suffering servant figure described by the prophet Isaiah (Isaiah 53:7), who will suffer death in order to take away the people's sins.

The high priest, Caiaphas, finally puts Jesus under oath in order to get him to respond. Caiaphas asks Jesus if he is the "Messiah, the Son of God" (26:63). Jesus could give a simple yes, but saying that he is the Son of God might be taken to mean that he is a king specially chosen by God (Psalm 2:7), and his identity as God's Son greatly exceeds such a narrow definition. Probably for this reason, Jesus refuses to answer directly. Jesus indicates that his role exceeds the establishment of a limited political kingdom by evoking the image of the "Son of Man," a heavenly figure involved in God's establishment of his reign on earth (Daniel 7:13—"one like a human being"). Jesus predicts that he will sit "at the right hand of Power" (26:64). Here, *Power* is a synonym for God, echoing Psalm 110:1. Thus Jesus tells the religious leaders judging him that he will ultimately share in the sovereignty and judgment of God. The high priest regards this as blasphemy, a judgment he dramatizes by tearing his clothing, a gesture of grief (compare 2 Samuel 1:11–12).

In condemning Jesus to death, the religious leaders condemn themselves. The declaration for which they convict Jesus is true. They have rejected their own Messiah.

Meanwhile, as Jesus endures interrogation inside the high priest's house, Peter faces a trial of his own in the courtyard. Both have their identities challenged; both are in danger, although Peter far less. While their situations are somewhat parallel, their responses could not be more different. Jesus proclaims his identity. Peter denies his, insisting repeatedly that he has nothing to do with Jesus. Peter reinforces his second and third denials with an oath—exactly the way of attesting that Jesus forbade his disciples to use (5:33–37), thus further emphasizing his disso-ciation from his master. Along with his denials, Peter even moves physically farther away from Jesus: the Greek indicates that Peter begins in the courtyard (26:69), withdraws to the "porch" (26:71), and finally goes out into the street (26:75). This scene, which ends in Peter's weeping bitter tears of repentance, is the last in which he is mentioned by name in Matthew's Gospel.

Peter's disloyalty to Jesus appears especially shameful here because of the important role Peter plays in Matthew's Gospel up to this point. Only Matthew describes Peter venturing out toward Jesus on the lake during a storm (14:28–33). Only Matthew describes Jesus singling Peter out as the recipient of a special revelation from God and being given the "keys of the kingdom" (16:17–19).

It is a mark of the honesty of the early Christians that they preserved this story of the tragic sin of one of their early leaders. They refused to whitewash their church history. Peter's denial of Jesus carried a powerful message for Matthew's first readers, as it does for us today.

Questions for Application

40 minutes
Choose questions according to your interest and time.

1 The religious leaders demand that Jesus explain himself, but it is difficult for him to reply to their questions directly without giving a misimpression. This points to the difficulty of understanding him. Why is it difficult to fully grasp who Jesus is? What aspects of Jesus' identity do you find hardest to understand? to explain to others?

2 In facing an unjust tribunal, Jesus makes what may seem to be an ineffective defense. Have you faced a trial or interrogation where the outcome seems predetermined? What kind of a defense did you make? What advice would you give to someone in these circumstances? How can a person tell whether it is better to be silent in the face of accusations or to speak?

3 Peter found himself in a situation where it was dangerous to acknowledge his friendship with Jesus. When have you been in a situation where it is awkward to acknowledge your relationship with Jesus? What can you learn from this situation?

4 When have you been embarrassed to acknowledge your relationship or friendship with another person? What did you do? How did your action affect your relationship with that person?

5 Peter's accent marked him as a Galilean, which led people in Jerusalem to suspect that he was associated with Jesus, who was also from Galilee. What is there about your lifestyle and behavior that marks you as a disciple of Jesus?

6 Besides denying Jesus verbally, as Peter did, what are other ways of denying Jesus?

7 For personal reflection: Matthew portrays Peter as a flawed man. The early Church, of which Peter was a leader, preserved this account. How might this help you ponder the condition of the Church in our own time?

If you disagree with someone else's comment, gently say so. Then explain your own point of view from the passage before you.

Paul E. Little, Christian Basics Bible Study series

Approach to Prayer

15 minutes
Use this approach—or create your own!

◆ Allow group members time to silently reflect on any situations that are causing suffering to them or to people they love. Then invite them to share a brief prayer, to the degree they are comfortable. Finally read aloud together the following prayer by St. Clare of Assisi, or ask one member to read it for the group.

Gaze upon him,
consider him,
contemplate him
as you desire to imitate him.
If you suffer with him, you will
    reign with him.
If you weep with him, you shall
    rejoice with him.
If you die with him on the cross
    of tribulation,
you shall possess heavenly
    mansions in the splendor of
    the saints,
and, in the Book of Life your
    name shall be called
    glorious among men.

Saints in the Making

A Prisoner's Hope

This section is a supplement for individual reading.

Francois-Xavier Cardinal Nguyen Van Thuan was born in French Indochina (today called Vietnam) in 1928. In 1967, he was named bishop of Nha Trang and then, in 1975, successor to the archbishop of Saigon (today called Ho Chi Minh City). On August 15, 1975, he was put under house arrest by the government and jailed more than a year later. He remained in some sort of confinement until 1991, when the Communist government expelled him from the country. He died in Rome in 2002.

As a prisoner, Archbishop Thuan spent nine years in isolation cells. During that time he managed to write and was even able to smuggle his writings out of his prisons and reeducation camps. He jotted the following notes the day after his arrest in 1975.

Jesus, yesterday afternoon, Feast of Mary Assumed, I was arrested. Taken during the night from Saigon to Nha Trang four hundred and fifty kilometers between two policemen, I began the experience of a prisoner's life. So many confused feelings in my head: sadness, fear, tension, my heart torn to pieces for being taken away from people. Humiliated, I remember the words of Sacred Scripture: "He let himself be taken for a criminal" [see Luke 22:37]. . . .

But in this sea of extreme bitterness, I feel freer than ever. I have nothing with me, not even a penny, except my rosary and the company of Jesus and Mary. Along the road of captivity, I prayed: You are my God and my all. . . .

The road of hope is paved with small steps of hope. The life of hope is made of brief minutes of hope. Like you, Jesus, who always did what was pleasing to your Father. Every minute I want to tell you: Jesus, I love you, my life is ever a "new and eternal covenant" with you. Every minute I want to sing with your Church: Glory to the Father and to the Son and to the Holy Spirit.

INNOCENT BLOOD

Questions to Begin

15 minutes
Use a question or two to get warmed up for the reading.

---

1 When was the last time you changed your mind about the wisdom of something you had already done?

---

2 How do you feel in a big crowd?
- ❑ I count the minutes until I can go out.
- ❑ I relax and just enjoy people-watching.
- ❑ I hang out at the concession stand.
- ❑ I join in whatever the crowd's doing.

5 minutes
Read the passage aloud. Let individuals take turns reading
paragraphs.

The Reading: Matthew 27:1–32

What Is That to Us?

1 When morning came, all the chief priests and the elders of the people conferred together against Jesus in order to bring about his death. 2 They bound him, led him away, and handed him over to Pilate the governor.

3 When Judas, his betrayer, saw that Jesus was condemned, he repented and brought back the thirty pieces of silver to the chief priests and the elders. 4 He said, "I have sinned by betraying innocent blood." But they said, "What is that to us? See to it yourself." 5 Throwing down the pieces of silver in the temple, he departed; and he went and hanged himself. 6 But the chief priests, taking the pieces of silver, said, "It is not lawful to put them into the treasury, since they are blood money." 7 After conferring together, they used them to buy the potter's field as a place to bury foreigners. 8 For this reason that field has been called the Field of Blood to this day. 9 Then was fulfilled what had been spoken through the prophet Jeremiah, "And they took the thirty pieces of silver, the price of the one on whom a price had been set, on whom some of the people of Israel had set a price, 10 and they gave them for the potter's field, as the Lord commanded me."

Crucify Him!

11 Now Jesus stood before the governor; and the governor asked him, "Are you the King of the Jews?" Jesus said, "You say so." 12 But when he was accused by the chief priests and elders, he did not answer. 13 Then Pilate said to him, "Do you not hear how many accusations they make against you?" 14 But he gave him no answer, not even to a single charge, so that the governor was greatly amazed.

15 Now at the festival the governor was accustomed to release a prisoner for the crowd, anyone whom they wanted. 16 At that time they had a notorious prisoner, called Jesus Barabbas. 17 So after they had gathered, Pilate said to them, "Whom do you want me to release for you, Jesus Barabbas or Jesus who is called the Messiah?" 18 For he realized that it was out of jealousy that they had handed him over.

[19] While he was sitting on the judgment seat, his wife sent word to him, "Have nothing to do with that innocent man, for today I have suffered a great deal because of a dream about him."

[20] Now the chief priests and the elders persuaded the crowds to ask for Barabbas and to have Jesus killed. [21] The governor again said to them, "Which of the two do you want me to release for you?" And they said, "Barabbas." [22] Pilate said to them, "Then what should I do with Jesus who is called the Messiah?" All of them said, "Let him be crucified!" [23] Then he asked, "Why, what evil has he done?" But they shouted all the more, "Let him be crucified!"

[24] So when Pilate saw that he could do nothing, but rather that a riot was beginning, he took some water and washed his hands before the crowd, saying, "I am innocent of this man's blood; see to it yourselves." [25] Then the people as a whole answered, "His blood be on us and on our children!" [26] So he released Barabbas for them; and after flogging Jesus, he handed him over to be crucified.

Hail, King of the Jews!

[27] Then the soldiers of the governor took Jesus into the governor's headquarters, and they gathered the whole cohort around him. [28] They stripped him and put a scarlet robe on him, [29] and after twisting some thorns into a crown, they put it on his head. They put a reed in his right hand and knelt before him and mocked him, saying, "Hail, King of the Jews!" [30] They spat on him, and took the reed and struck him on the head. [31] After mocking him, they stripped him of the robe and put his own clothes on him. Then they led him away to crucify him.

[32] As they went out, they came upon a man from Cyrene named Simon; they compelled this man to carry his cross.

10 minutes
Choose questions according to your interest and time.

1 Previously in this Gospel, Jesus criticized the Pharisees for paying more attention to the details rather than the larger spirit of the law. How do the religious authorities' actions in this passage reflect Jesus' criticism of religious people who "strain out a gnat but swallow a camel" (23:24)?

2 What similarities and differences are there between Judas's and Peter's responses to their own remorse?

3 Why was Pilate "amazed" (27:14)?

4 Why do the soldiers make a crown out of thorns for Jesus (27:29)?

5 How does Matthew highlight Jesus' innocence in this passage?

A Guide to the Reading

If participants have not read this section already, read it aloud. Otherwise go on to "Questions for Application."

27:1–32. Matthew returns to Judas in this chapter, presenting him as a contrast to Peter and using him to underline Jesus' innocence. Judas makes his decision to return the money when he sees the consequences of his actions for Jesus. Didn't he realize that if he betrayed Jesus to them, the temple authorities would have Jesus put to death? Judas recognizes that taking "innocent blood" is an especially heinous crime that merits a curse (Deuteronomy 27:25). Judas "repented" (27:3)—the Greek word means "to change one's mind." (This translation of the Greek is used in 21:29, 32.) But he has not grasped Jesus' message of forgiveness. In sorrow for denying Jesus, Peter "went out and wept bitterly" (26:75). After changing his mind about betraying Jesus, Judas "went and hanged himself" (27:5).

The religious leaders admit that they cannot put the money in the temple treasury because it is "blood money" (27:6). This admission underlines their corruption. They implicitly acknowledge Jesus' innocence, yet express more concern about the ritual defilement of the temple treasury than about the grave sin of killing an innocent person.

Judas' earnings are used to purchase a plot of land where foreigners will be buried. Matthew alludes to a statement by the prophet Jeremiah (27:9–10—actually he combines words from Jeremiah and Zechariah) to provide yet one more piece of evidence that Jesus' death fulfilled ancient prophecies and thus, despite all appearances, was mysteriously consistent with God's plan.

Jesus appears before Pilate, and the blasphemy charge has now been replaced by a more political accusation. Prompted no doubt by the temple authorities, Pilate asks Jesus if he is the "King of the Jews" (27:11). An affirmative answer would be an admission of sedition. In the sense that Pilate understands the term, it would also be untrue. While Jesus *is* the promised king of Israel, he is not the kind of king that Pilate has in mind. As he did before his previous questioners, Jesus refuses to answer Pilate directly. His "You say so" (27:11) is his last utterance until the cross—his silence again bringing to mind the patiently suffering servant spoken of by Isaiah (Isaiah 52:13–53:12), the mysterious figure who would, by his suffering, reconcile humanity to God.

Jesus was a common name in first-century Palestine, so it is not surprising that a criminal in Jerusalem bears the same name. Jesus Barabbas was probably an insurrectionist (Luke 23:19). We can be sure that the irony of the criminal's other name, Barabbas, which means "son of the father," was not lost on Matthew and his first readers. In choosing to save the life of a political rebel who is the son of an earthly father, the crowd rejects the Messiah, the Son of the heavenly Father, who calls them into his eternal kingdom.

Throughout his Gospel, Matthew has highlighted the fact that gentiles as well as Jews will have a place in God's kingdom. Matthew portrays non-Jews who were more open to Jesus than some of his own people. A case in point is Pilate's wife, who calls her husband's attention to the insight she has derived from a dream. Jesus' life was saved at the beginning of Matthew's Gospel in part through dreams given to gentiles (2:12); now his life could be saved again by the same means. Pilate seems willing to release Jesus. But then, in his weakness, he gives in to the crowd, which is encouraged by the religious leaders to seek Jesus' death (27:20, 23–24). Pilate makes a symbolic gesture—washing his hands—as a sign of absolving himself of responsibility. Whether he thus escaped responsibility for the crime of Jesus' death is questionable, but his action further underlines Jesus' innocence. Even the judge who condemned Jesus recognized that Jesus had done nothing wrong.

In the end, Matthew presents a tragic scene. An innocent man is put to death, and virtually every actor in the drama proves unable to distinguish between good and evil, truth and falsehood, blessing and curse—or is unable to stand up for what is right. It is a narrative in which we can catch sight of ourselves at every turn. We, too, are confused about right and wrong. We, too, do the wrong thing, and then regret it. We persist in doing wrong although we know what is right. We allow ourselves to be pressured and led astray. We let evil triumph. In this story, we see the price that is paid for our betrayal of truth.

Questions for Application

40 minutes
Choose questions according to your interest and time.

1 What was lacking in Judas's repentance? What are the elements of true repentance? (See the *Catechism of the Catholic Church*, sections 1430–32.) What helps you to repent of sin?

2 The implication of Matthew's account is that Judas didn't believe he could be forgiven. What would you tell Judas—or anyone who thinks this?

3 Pilate knew better than to condemn Jesus. He saw the wicked motives of the religious leaders. His own wife warned him. Have you ever issued a warning that was ignored, or brushed aside a warning from someone else? What did you learn from this situation?

4 Pilate gave in to pressure to do something that was against his better judgment. When have you given in to pressure from others to do something you thought was unwise or wrong? What helps a person resist such pressures?

5 Pilate's washing his hands has become proverbial for disowning responsibility for a situation. When have you washed your hands of a responsibility and later regretted it? How would you handle the situation differently if you faced it again?

6 Jesus is not only tortured but also mocked. How does mockery affect a person? Is there a situation in your life where you could act to eliminate or counteract the mockery that someone is suffering?

Assume that personal information spoken within the group setting is private, unless you are specifically told otherwise.

Paul E. Little, Christian Basics Bible Study series

Approach to Prayer

15 minutes
Use this approach—or create your own!

♦ Invite members of the group to share any news or thoughts related to the prayers they offered last week for those in their lives who were suffering. Take a few moments to pray for their situations again, or for any new concerns that have arisen in the past week. Then ask a member of the group to read Philippians 2:5–11 aloud. After a short period of silence, end by praying the Our Father together.

A Living Tradition

Now I Am Becoming a Disciple!

This section is a supplement for individual reading.

Many Christians have endured martyrdom. One of the most prominent martyrs in the Church's early years was Ignatius, bishop of Antioch (modern Antakya, Turkey). There, government authorities arrested him and took him in chains to be executed in Rome. Along the way, he wrote letters to seven Christian communities, giving us a vivid picture of a soul who, out of the deepest faith, joined his own suffering to the suffering of Christ. His letter to the Christians in Rome reflects the harsh reality that Ignatius expects to face when he arrives there: literally, being fed to animals for the entertainment of a Roman crowd.

I am wheat for God, being ground by the teeth of wild animals to become a pure loaf for Christ. . . . Pray to Christ for me that by these means I may become a sacrifice. I do not give you commands, like Peter and Paul. They were apostles; I am a condemned man. They were free men; I am, up to the present moment, a slave. But if I suffer, I shall become a freedman of Jesus Christ and, in him, I will rise up free.

At the moment, in chains, I am learning to give up all desires. From Syria to Rome, by land and sea, night and day I am fighting with wild beasts, chained to ten leopards—I mean the detachment of soldiers!—who only get worse the better they are treated. But by the injuries they inflict I am becoming a better disciple. . . . In fact, now I am beginning to be a disciple. . . .

May nothing seen or unseen prevent me from gaining Jesus Christ. Fire, cross, combat with wild beasts, cutting and wrenching, crushing of bones, dismemberment, grinding up of the whole body, fiendish torments—let them come! Only let me gain Jesus Christ! . . . He is the one I am seeking—the one who died for us. He is the one I desire—the one who rose for us. . . .

Let me take possession of the pure light, for only when I get there will I truly be human. So let me imitate the suffering of my God!

GOLGOTHA

Questions to Begin

15 minutes
Use a question or two to get warmed up for the reading.

1 When did someone do something good that helped you see them in a new light?

2 Describe a situation in which another person helped you in an unexpected way.

3 What does it feel like to be in the middle of an earthquake or a huge storm?

5 minutes
Read the passage aloud. Let individuals take turns reading
paragraphs.

The Reading: Matthew 27:33–66

This Is Jesus, King of the Jews

33 And when they came to a place called Golgotha (which means
Place of a Skull), 34 they offered him wine to drink, mixed with gall;
but when he tasted it, he would not drink it. 35 And when they had
crucified him, they divided his clothes among themselves by casting
lots; 36 then they sat down there and kept watch over him. 37 Over his
head they put the charge against him, which read, "This is Jesus, the
King of the Jews."

38 Then two bandits were crucified with him, one on his right
and one on his left. 39 Those who passed by derided him, shaking
their heads 40 and saying, "You who would destroy the temple and
build it in three days, save yourself! If you are the Son of God, come
down from the cross." 41 In the same way the chief priests also, along
with the scribes and elders, were mocking him, saying, 42 "He saved
others; he cannot save himself. He is the King of Israel; let him come
down from the cross now, and we will believe in him. 43 He trusts in
God; let God deliver him now, if he wants to; for he said, 'I am God's
Son.'" 44 The bandits who were crucified with him also taunted him
in the same way.

Jesus Breathes His Last

45 From noon on, darkness came over the whole land until three in
the afternoon. 46 And about three o'clock Jesus cried with a loud
voice, "Eli, Eli, lema sabachthani?" that is, "My God, my God, why
have you forsaken me?" 47 When some of the bystanders heard it,
they said, "This man is calling for Elijah." 48 At once one of them
ran and got a sponge, filled it with sour wine, put it on a stick, and
gave it to him to drink. 49 But the others said, "Wait, let us see
whether Elijah will come to save him." 50 Then Jesus cried again
with a loud voice and breathed his last. 51 At that moment the
curtain of the temple was torn in two, from top to bottom. The earth
shook, and the rocks were split. 52 The tombs also were opened, and
many bodies of the saints who had fallen asleep were raised. 53 After
his resurrection they came out of the tombs and entered the holy city
and appeared to many. 54 Now when the centurion and those with

him, who were keeping watch over Jesus, saw the earthquake and what took place, they were terrified and said, "Truly this man was God's Son!"

55 Many women were also there, looking on from a distance; they had followed Jesus from Galilee and had provided for him. 56 Among them were Mary Magdalene, and Mary the mother of James and Joseph, and the mother of the sons of Zebedee.

Sealing the Tomb

57 When it was evening, there came a rich man from Arimathea, named Joseph, who was also a disciple of Jesus. 58 He went to Pilate and asked for the body of Jesus; then Pilate ordered it to be given to him. 59 So Joseph took the body and wrapped it in a clean linen cloth 60 and laid it in his own new tomb, which he had hewn in the rock. He then rolled a great stone to the door of the tomb and went away. 61 Mary Magdalene and the other Mary were there, sitting opposite the tomb.

62 The next day, that is, after the day of Preparation, the chief priests and the Pharisees gathered before Pilate 63 and said, "Sir, we remember what that impostor said while he was still alive, 'After three days I will rise again.' 64 Therefore command the tomb to be made secure until the third day; otherwise his disciples may go and steal him away, and tell the people, 'He has been raised from the dead,' and the last deception would be worse than the first." 65 Pilate said to them, "You have a guard of soldiers; go, make it as secure as you can." 66 So they went with the guard and made the tomb secure by sealing the stone.

Questions for Careful Reading

10 minutes
Choose questions according to your interest and time.

1 What is the common thread in the people's mockery of Jesus? Consider also last week's reading.

2 What does the reader of this passage know that the witnesses of Jesus' crucifixion do not? How does this knowledge affect how the reader views their mockery?

3 Who in this passage recognizes Jesus' true identity? What might be the significance of Jesus' recognition by these people?

4 If, after Jesus' resurrection, people spread a rumor that his body had been stolen by his disciples, what details in this passage would serve to refute this allegation?

A Guide to the Reading

If participants have not read this section already, read it aloud. Otherwise go on to "Questions for Application."

27:33–66. The crucifixion of Jesus seems inescapably to evoke such feelings of sadness that they threaten to outweigh the great hope his death holds for us. Even though we know that the story ends in triumph, even though we have two thousand years of theological reflection to help us put Jesus' death in perspective, still the Crucifixion remains shocking and even baffling.

The good things of life in this world are great gifts of God. How could he strip these blessings away from his own Son, allowing him to suffer a cruel, unjust death? How could *this* be God's chosen means of overcoming sin and drawing the human race to himself? At the cross, we confront a profound mystery. Matthew knew this, and he wrote his narrative of Jesus' crucifixion to help us believe, despite the mystery, that in Jesus' death, God was truly at work.

The Roman government reserved crucifixion for violent criminals, traitors, and rebellious slaves. It was a hideous death, in which the victim suffered for hours, even days, hanging naked in public, tied or nailed to wooden beams. Matthew did not have to describe it in detail. His readers knew how crucifixion worked and perhaps had even witnessed it. Those who were Jews also knew that Mosaic Law maintained that those who died in this manner were especially cursed (Deuteronomy 21:22–23). How, then, could a crucified man be the messiah?

Matthew gives his answer by the way he tells the story of Jesus' death. Repeatedly he shows how the events of Jesus' passion echo Scripture. Matthew recounts the death of Jesus in words that echo scriptural passages about God's chosen one being "rejected" (Isaiah 53:3), mocked (Psalm 22:7), scourged (Isaiah 53:5), and pierced (Isaiah 53:4). He reminds us of passages that foreshadowed his tormenters' sharing out his garments (Psalm 22:18), his silent endurance (Isaiah 53:7), yet also his crying out to God from the depths of his pain (Psalm 22:1). Matthew's scriptural allusions do not explain the mystery of Jesus' suffering, but they carry the message that his suffering was foreseen in the divine plan. They assure the reader that people's rejection of Jesus could not prevent God from achieving his purposes.

Matthew's Jewish readers valued Scripture as God's word. For them, the allusions to the prophets and the psalms demonstrated that Jesus' death was not evidence that his claims about himself were false. Jesus' death was, in fact, consistent with the plan of God, who intended to bring the forgiveness of sins through the suffering of his sinless Son (26:28; compare Isaiah 53:11).

Throughout his narrative of Jesus' suffering, Matthew highlights the tragic irony of the charges against Jesus. The Roman soldiers mock him as "King of the Jews" (27:29), and those same words are written as a cruel joke on the sign posted above his head. On the cross, Jesus is subjected to the jibes of passersby challenging him to come down from the cross and save himself if all he says about his relationship with God is true. Jesus is indeed the royal Messiah. He does have the power to come down from the cross. The mystery, as Scripture scholar John Meier writes, is that "the enemies of Jesus see his sufferings as proof that he is not God's Son; Matthew sees them as proof that he is."

After Jesus dies, God's power shows the mockery and contempt of Jesus' tormenters for the foolishness that it is. Darkness falls—a sign of judgment. The earth shakes. The curtain hiding the inner sanctuary of the temple splits, symbolizing the gift of a new intimacy with God through Jesus' sacrifice. These signs reveal the truth: the power that Jesus exercised during his ministry was, indeed, *God's* power. Among the first to recognize this is a Roman soldier standing watch, a gentile, who gasps in amazement: "Truly this man was God's Son!" (27:54).

The terrible day ends quietly. A man named Joseph, who is identified in Mark's Gospel as a member of the temple council (Mark 15:43), takes Jesus' lifeless body and quickly lays it in a tomb. As some women who accompanied Jesus from Galilee watch, Joseph rolls a stone across the mouth of the burial cave. Pilate agrees to the religious leaders' request to seal the stone and post a guard.

This, it seems, is the end of Jesus of Nazareth.

Questions for Application

40 minutes
Choose questions according to your interest and time.

---

1 Those who mock Jesus seem to believe that if God is really present in a situation, he will quickly correct injustice and prevent innocent suffering. When have you been tempted to wonder if God is really present in a situation of injustice or suffering? How have you dealt with this question?

---

2 What are the signs of God's presence? What does it mean when these signs seem to be lacking?

---

3 What does it mean to trust God in the midst of suffering: to believe that he has caused the suffering? to believe that he will end the suffering? to believe that he will act through the suffering? What can be learned about God's view of suffering from Matthew's account of Jesus' passion?

---

4 Jesus is finally recognized as God's Son as he experiences the ultimate human weakness— death. What does this suggest about the value of human life in its weakest conditions? What does it suggest about God's relationship to us in our times of weakness?

5 When has someone accepted suffering out of love for you? When have you accepted suffering out of love for someone else? What effect have these experiences had on your life?

6 At the cross, some women offer Jesus the support of their presence (27:55–56). When have you received quiet support from another person in a difficult time? How did that help you? What opportunity do you have now to be a quiet support to someone who is suffering?

7 For personal reflection: Are you afraid of dying? Why or why not? What does this reading say to you about fear of death? What does it mean for you that Jesus died for you?

Don't be afraid of controversy. It can be very stimulating. Differences can enrich our lives.

Dale and Juanita Ryan, Letting God Be God Bible Study series

Approach to Prayer

15 minutes
Use this approach—or create your own!

◆ Set up a crucifix in the room where you are meeting so that everyone may use it as a visual focus for prayer. Take a few moments to quietly contemplate the crucifix. Then pray Psalm 22 together, perhaps by dividing into two groups that take turns reading verses.

Saints in the Making

The Marks of Jesus' Suffering

This section is a supplement for individual reading

Christians' sharing in Jesus' suffering takes many forms. This aspect of discipleship involves patiently enduring pain and loss that come as a result of following Jesus, while asking God to bring good from it. It involves accepting mockery, rejection, or worse, rather than betraying God's love.

Paul drew a connection between bearing suffering in his ministry and sharing the suffering of Jesus when he wrote to the Christians in Galatia that "I carry the marks of Jesus branded on my body" (Galatians 6:17). Visionaries and mystics in the centuries since have experienced their own physical suffering as a way of participating in the suffering of Christ. In a few cases, sharing in Jesus' suffering has even involved literally bearing the physical marks of Jesus' suffering. The term for these marks is *stigmata,* derived from a Latin word meaning "marks."

The first and best-known person to bear the stigmata was the Italian saint Francis of Assisi (1181–1226). He received the stigmata near the end of his life, in 1224, when he was in deep contemplation. A Franciscan narrative, *The Little Flowers of St. Francis,* written about a hundred years after his death, tells the story.

St. Francis, sometime before dawn, began to pray outside . . . turning his face toward the east. And he prayed in this way: "My Lord Jesus Christ, I pray you to grant me two graces before I die: the first is that during my life I may feel in my soul and in my body, as much as possible, that pain which you, dear Jesus, sustained in the hour of your most bitter passion. The second is that I may feel in my heart, as much as possible, that excessive love with which you, O Son of God, were inflamed in willingly enduring such suffering for us sinners." . . .

St. Francis began to contemplate with intense devotion the passion of Christ and his infinite charity. And the fervor of his devotion increased so much within him that he utterly transformed himself into Jesus through love and compassion. . . . It left a most intense ardor and flame of divine love in the heart of St. Francis, and it left a marvelous image and imprint of the passion of Christ in his flesh. For soon there began to appear in the hands and feet of St. Francis the marks of nails such as he had just seen in the body of Jesus crucified.

ALLELUIA!

Questions to Begin

15 minutes
Use a question or two to get warmed up for the reading.

1 What's the closest you ever got to lightning?

2 When given a task by another person, what do you do?
❑ I follow instructions to the letter.
❑ I combine their ideas and my own.
❑ I pretty much go my own way.

5 minutes
*Read the passage aloud. Let individuals take turns reading
paragraphs.*

The Reading: Matthew 28

Do Not Be Afraid

[1] After the sabbath, as the first day of the week was dawning, Mary
Magdalene and the other Mary went to see the tomb. [2] And
suddenly there was a great earthquake; for an angel of the Lord,
descending from heaven, came and rolled back the stone and sat on
it. [3] His appearance was like lightning, and his clothing white as
snow. [4] For fear of him the guards shook and became like dead men.
[5] But the angel said to the women, "Do not be afraid; I know that
you are looking for Jesus who was crucified. [6] He is not here; for he
has been raised, as he said. Come, see the place where he lay. [7] Then
go quickly and tell his disciples, 'He has been raised from the dead,
and indeed he is going ahead of you to Galilee; there you will see
him.' This is my message for you." [8] So they left the tomb quickly
with fear and great joy, and ran to tell his disciples. [9] Suddenly Jesus
met them and said, "Greetings!" And they came to him, took hold
of his feet, and worshiped him. [10] Then Jesus said to them, "Do not
be afraid; go and tell my brothers to go to Galilee; there they will
see me."

Planting Rumors

[11] While they were going, some of the guard went into the city and
told the chief priests everything that had happened. [12] After the
priests had assembled with the elders, they devised a plan to give a
large sum of money to the soldiers, [13] telling them, "You must say,
'His disciples came by night and stole him away while we were
asleep.' [14] If this comes to the governor's ears, we will satisfy him
and keep you out of trouble." [15] So they took the money and did as
they were directed. And this story is still told among the Jews to
this day.

A New Beginning

16 Now the eleven disciples went to Galilee, to the mountain to which Jesus had directed them. 17 When they saw him, they worshiped him; but some doubted. 18 And Jesus came and said to them, "All authority in heaven and on earth has been given to me. 19 Go therefore and make disciples of all nations, baptizing them in the name of the Father and of the Son and of the Holy Spirit, 20 and teaching them to obey everything that I have commanded you. And remember, I am with you always, to the end of the age."

10 minutes
Choose questions according to your interest and time.

1 Reread 28:2. At what previous point in our readings from Matthew did the earth shake? What do these two incidents have in common?

2 At what other points in our readings did women appear? Putting these incidents together, how would you describe the women's role in the events of Jesus' death and resurrection?

3 Why are the guards afraid? Why are the women afraid? Does the angel address the women's fears?

4 After talking with the angel, the women are still afraid (28:8). Is it the same kind of fear they experienced before the angel's message?

5 The women are not only afraid but also joyful (28:8). How could that be?

6 The angel and Jesus send the women to tell the male disciples about Jesus' resurrection. Do the disciples believe the women's report?

A Guide to the Reading

*If participants have not read this section already, read it aloud.
Otherwise go on to "Questions for Application."*

28. As this final chapter of Matthew's Gospel begins, the Sabbath
has passed. It is very early Sunday morning. Two women—Mary
Magdalene and another Mary, who were present when Jesus was
crucified and buried—return to the tomb. In the culture of the time,
it was common for family members and friends to return to the
tomb of a deceased person for several days after burial.

As on the afternoon when Jesus died, the earth trembles,
manifesting a kind of awareness of a momentous act by God. An
angel moves away the stone that blocks the entrance to Jesus'
tomb, revealing that the tomb is empty. Be not afraid, he tells the
astonished women. These words concern not only the situation of
the moment, which was enough to frighten anyone, as the reaction
of the guards shows; the angel's call to put aside fear has a wider
application: be not afraid, for death has been conquered.

The women are the first to hear the good news of Jesus'
resurrection. The fact that they play such a key role is in
keeping with the way Jesus conducted his ministry. He invited
all people to be reconciled to God and prepare to enter his kingdom. He directed his attention especially to those who were
weak or sick, who were outsiders or of low social standing, who
were ritually unclean according to Mosaic Law. Women did not
play a central role in public events in Jewish society. Yet it is
now two women who are the first to learn of Jesus' triumph over
death. Jesus, executed by the powerful, first reveals the joy of
his resurrection to the powerless.

The women's role is, in fact, evidence for the truthfulness
of the account. If Jesus' followers had fabricated the claim that he
rose from the dead, it would have been senseless for them to make
women the first witnesses, for a woman's word was considered
less trustworthy than that of a man. A woman's testimony did not
have equal weight with a man's testimony in a court of law.

Matthew cannot end his Gospel without contrasting once
more the Jewish religious leaders and Jesus. Both send their
followers out to spread news. The temple authorities pay their
followers to spread a lie, while Jesus sends out his disciples to
spread the truth. The scene underlines for the last time the temple

officials' unyielding close-mindedness and their resistance to God's action. They continue to oppose Jesus despite all the evidence.

Jesus sends his disciples forth in their ministry from Galilee, where his ministry began. This implies that they are to carry on his work. He began in Galilee to preach that God's kingdom was near; his disciples are now to go out from Galilee telling the whole world that the kingdom has begun to arrive in Jesus' death and resurrection. Risen from the dead, Jesus' identity now shines forth clearly. He is not just a wise teacher but the one to whom "all authority" (28:18) has been given by God. With this divine authority he sends the disciples out to spread the good news of forgiveness and eternal life.

This is not the first time Jesus has sent his disciples forth. Earlier he sent them to the villages of Galilee to cast out evil spirits and to heal every kind of illness—but he did not include teaching in their commission (10:1). Now he sends them out to make disciples of all people, teaching them everything that he has taught. Why the change in their commission? The difference is that now they have witnessed the fullness of the Good News. During his ministry, Jesus alerted them to the fact that his mission entailed suffering, but the disciples never seemed to want to hear that part of his instruction. Now they have witnessed his death. They have seen the scope of his love. And they have experienced the forgiveness, hope, and peace of his resurrection. They have learned that along the way to God's kingdom suffering must play a part. And they have seen that God overcomes all suffering and evil in the resurrection of his Son. Knowing all this, they are ready to communicate Jesus' teaching to the whole world.

Jesus assures them that as they go, they are not alone. He will be with them—and with us—always.

Questions for Application

40 minutes
Choose questions according to your interest and time.

1 Both the angel and Jesus tell the women not to be afraid. Is it possible not to be afraid of death? How? What does the final reading from Matthew offer to answer these questions?

2 Put yourself in the place of a disciple hearing about Jesus' resurrection for the first time. How might this change the way the disciple views Jesus' entire life? How might it change the way the disciple views his or her own life? How might it change the way you look at your life?

3 In 28:17 we read that the disciples "worshiped him; but some doubted." Is doubt inevitably part of Christian life? How can our doubts play a constructive role in our faith life? How do you deal with doubts?

4 Even with our faith in the promise of eternal life, is there room for grief and sadness concerning death?

5 The passage ends with Jesus' command to go forth to all nations with the Good News. What is your part in this great project? Are you giving it your full efforts?

6 What is the most important thing you will take away from your reading about Jesus' suffering and resurrection? How will it change the way you respond to God's grace?

Periods of silence don't always have to be filled immediately. Allow members time to digest what they are discovering.

Gladys M. Hunt, *You Can Start a Bible Study Group*

Approach to Prayer

15 minutes
Use this approach—or create your own!

◆ Invite group members to share prayers of thanksgiving to God. End by praying this excerpt from the *Exsultet,* the hymn that is sung at the vigil liturgy on the night before Easter Sunday.

Rejoice, heavenly powers!
Sing, choirs of angels!
    Exult, all creation around
    God's throne!
    Jesus Christ our king is
    risen!
    Sound the trumpet of
    salvation! . . .
Glory fills you!
    Darkness vanishes for
    ever! . . .
The power of this holy night
    dispels all evil,
    washes guilt away,
restores lost innocence,
    brings mourners joy.
    It casts out hatred,
brings us peace,
    and humbles earthly pride.
Night truly blessed,
    when heaven is wedded to
    earth
    and we are reconciled to
    God!

A Living Tradition

Easter Joy

This section is a supplement for individual reading.

St. John Chrysostom (AD 347–407) was archbishop of Constantinople, the city now known as Istanbul, Turkey. His vigorous, brilliant preaching earned him the name by which we now call him, Chrysostom, which means "golden mouthed." This Easter homily, delivered around AD 400 and still read at Orthodox Easter liturgies, gives an impression of his gift.

Is there anyone who is a devout lover of God?
Let them enjoy this beautiful bright festival!
Is there anyone who is a grateful servant?
Let them rejoice and enter into the joy of their Lord! . . .

Let us all enter into the joy of the Lord!
First and last alike receive your reward;
rich and poor, rejoice together!
Sober and slothful, celebrate the day! . . .

Let no one grieve at his poverty,
for the universal kingdom has been revealed.
Let no one mourn that he has fallen again and again;
for forgiveness has risen from the grave.
Let no one fear death, for the Death of our Savior has set us free.
He has destroyed it by enduring it. . . .

O death, where is thy sting?
O Hades, where is thy victory?

Christ is Risen, and you, o death, are annihilated!
Christ is Risen, and the evil ones are cast down!
Christ is Risen, and the angels rejoice!
Christ is Risen, and life is liberated!
Christ is Risen, and the tomb is emptied of its dead;
for Christ having risen from the dead,
is become the first-fruits of those who have fallen asleep.

So Tenderly Loved

In every century, Christians have reflected on this profound mystery: the death of Jesus on the cross repairs this broken world, bringing wholeness out of our own brokenness. Here are two brief examples of such spiritual reflection.

The first is from St. Francis de Sales (1567–1622), who was bishop of Geneva, Switzerland, and a well-known spiritual director. His writings on the spiritual life were unusual at the time because he included laypeople in his audience. His *Introduction to the Devout Life,* from which this excerpt was taken, draws on his advice to an actual French woman but is addressed to a fictional female character called Philothea, or "one who loves God."

Consider the love with which our dear Lord Jesus Christ bore so much in this world, especially in the Garden of Olives and on Mount Calvary. That love bore you in mind, and through all those pains and toils he obtained your good resolutions for you, as also all that is needful to maintain, foster, strengthen, and consummate those resolutions. How precious must the resolutions be which are the fruits of our Lord's passion! And how dear to my heart, since they were dear to that of Jesus! ("Savior of my soul, you died to win them for me; grant me grace sooner to die than forget them!")

Be sure, my daughter, that the heart of our most dear Lord beheld you from the tree of the cross and loved you, and by that love he won for you all good things which you will ever have, and among them your good resolutions. . . . A woman with child makes ready for the babe she expects, prepares its cradle, its swaddling clothes, and its nurse. Even so our Lord, while hanging on his cross, prepared all that you could need for your happiness, all the means, the graces, the leadings by which he leads your soul onwards toward perfection.

Surely we ought ever to remember this, and ask fervently: Is it possible that I was loved, and loved so tenderly by my savior, that he should have thought of me individually, in all these details by which he has drawn me to himself? With what love and gratitude ought I to use all he has given me? The loving heart of my God thought of my soul, loved it, and prepared endless means to promote its salvation, as though there were no other soul on earth of which he thought, just as the sun shines on each spot of earth as brightly as though it shone nowhere else but reserved all its brightness for that alone. So our dear Lord thought and cared for every one of his children as though none other existed. "Who loved me, and gave himself for me," St. Paul says (Galatians 2:20), as though he meant, "for me alone, as if there were none but me he cared for."

Let this be engraved on your soul, my child, the better to cherish and foster your good resolutions, which are so precious to the heart of Jesus.

Father Richard John Neuhaus, a priest in New York City, is well-known as a writer and editor. He wrote an extended meditation on Jesus' suffering, *Death on a Friday Afternoon,* after serious illness brought him close to death.

Even as he penetrates into the heart of darkness, Jesus is not abandoned by the light. . . . And his penetrating into the heart of darkness means that nobody, absolutely nobody is alone in the heart of darkness. Christ has been there, Christ is there. From the cross point of history the word goes out that those who think they are abandoned by God are in fact not abandoned. We can despair of God, but he never despairs of us. We can turn our back upon God, but he never turns his back upon us. Never! There is absolutely nobody seated on the long mourners' bench of the eternal pity who is in a place where Jesus has not been before, where he is not now. This is what it means to find ourselves at the foot of the cross. . . . At the foot of the cross, faith discerns, through our tears, that nothing is left unattended, nothing unknown, nothing unloved, nothing unredeemed.

Atonement. The Great Thing, the thing that had to be done or else nothing could be done, has been done. On a certain Friday afternoon at about three o'clock, when the children were coming home from school, when the Lamb of God cried, "It is finished.". . . How strange that in this end should be our beginning.

Jesus' Death and the Jewish People

Matthew gives a very negative portrayal of the Jewish leaders, and even the other Jewish inhabitants of Jerusalem, in the process of Jesus' condemnation and death. Through the centuries, many Christians have found in Matthew's account a basis for believing that Jews in general are guilty of Jesus' death. A careful examination of Matthew's Gospel, however, reveals that his account of Jesus' death does not justify this view.

A council chaired by the high priest that ruled over Jerusalem was not representative of the Jewish people of the time. The council members belonged to a social and economic elite. They were able to occupy their position of power only because the Roman government allowed them to do so with the understanding that they would maintain order and protect Roman interests. The high priests were chosen directly by the Roman government, and loyalty to the Roman regime was an important prerequisite for the appointment.

The temple authorities, then, had not only religious but also political and economic reasons for rejecting Jesus. Jesus threatened their social and economic prerogatives. The enthusiasm of the crowds of Jesus' admirers posed a threat of disorder and even rebellion against the Roman authorities. Thus the temple leaders' conspiracy against Jesus did not represent a rejection of Jesus by the Jewish people of the time. Indeed, the openness of many of their fellow Jews to Jesus was one of the main reasons the religious leaders wanted to get rid of him.

Matthew's portrayal of these Jewish religious leaders in a harsh light should not be taken as an expression of anti-Jewishness on his part. Every indication is that Matthew, like Jesus and all his first followers, was a Jew. In highlighting the religious leaders' wickedness and resistance to God, Matthew stands in a long Jewish tradition of prophets who sharply condemned the blindness and injustices of bad leaders of the people of Israel. Matthew is not an outsider condemning Judaism. He is an insider who sees a strong historical precedent for interpreting a situation in light of God's revelation and for criticizing those who reject God's action.

One moment in Matthew's Gospel stands out as particularly problematic in its picture of ordinary Jews. It is the cry of the crowd, "His blood be on us and on our children!" (27:25). These words express utter rejection of Jesus, absolute refusal to perceive him as the Messiah whom God has sent. Matthew shows that this attitude was tragically wrong. While there are complexities to this passage that cannot be discussed here, two important considerations may be noted that prevent us from reading Matthew's report of this scene as his way of expressing the view that the Jewish people have placed themselves under God's judgment.

One consideration is that throughout his Gospel, Matthew shows that crowds of Jewish people are consistently favorable toward Jesus throughout his ministry, even up to the final days when he arrives in Jerusalem for the Passover. Only on this occasion does a Jewish crowd turn against Jesus, and on this occasion they are persuaded to do so by the "chief priests and the elders" (27:20). Thus the crowds' demand for Jesus' death only highlights the responsibility of the temple authorities, who were even able to lead the generally sympathetic crowds to turn against Jesus.

A second consideration is that the crowd is not authorized to speak on behalf of all Jews. Nowhere in Matthew's Gospel does Jesus support the idea of guilt by association. Jesus makes it clear that no one will be rewarded for living in the same town with him or even for being one of his relatives: each person must bear their own responsibility for deciding whether to accept or reject him. Each person will ultimately be judged on the basis of their own choices. This assumption of the principle of individual responsibility and judgment underlies all of Jesus' preaching to individuals, inviting them to follow him and learn his ways. Thus the idea that a crowd of Jews in Jerusalem could bring judgment upon Jews elsewhere or upon Jews of any later time is foreign to the outlook of Matthew's Gospel.

Quite simply, only those who participated in the conspiracy against Jesus were guilty of his death. The vast majority of Jews at the time had no responsibility for it. No Jews of other times or places bear any responsibility whatsoever for Jesus' death. Christians who have thought that later Jews share the blame for Jesus' death have been very seriously mistaken.

Suggestions for Bible Discussion Groups

L ike a camping trip, a Bible discussion group works best if you agree on where you're going and how you intend to get there. Many groups use their first meeting to talk over such questions. Here is a checklist of issues, with bits of advice from people who have experience in Bible discussions. (A planning discussion will go more smoothly if the leaders have thought through the following issues beforehand.)

Agree on your purpose. Are you getting together to gain wisdom and direction for your lives? to finally get acquainted with the Bible? to support one another in following Christ? to encourage those who are exploring—or reexploring—the Church? for other reasons?

Agree on attitudes. For example: "We're all beginners here." "We're here to help one another understand and respond to God's word." "We're not here to offer counseling or direction to each other." "We want to read Scripture prayerfully." What do *you* wish to emphasize? Make it explicit!

Agree on ground rules. Barbara J. Fleischer, in her useful book *Facilitating for Growth,* recommends that a group clearly state its approach to the following:

- ◆ *Preparation.* Do we agree to read the material and prepare the answers to the questions before each meeting?
- ◆ *Attendance.* What kind of priority will we give to our meetings?
- ◆ *Self-revelation.* Are we willing to help the others in the group gradually get to know us—our weaknesses as well as our strengths, our needs as well as our gifts?
- ◆ *Listening.* Will we commit ourselves to listen to one another?
- ◆ *Confidentiality.* Will we keep everything that is shared *with* the group *in* the group?
- ◆ *Discretion.* Will we refrain from sharing about the faults and sins of people who are not in the group?
- ◆ *Encouragement and support.* Will we give as well as receive?
- ◆ *Participation.* Will we give each person the time and opportunity to make a contribution?

You could probably take a pen and draw a circle around *listening* and *confidentiality.* Those two points are especially important.

The following items could be added to Fleischer's list:

◆ *Relationship with parish.* Is our group part of the adult faith-formation program? independent but operating with the express approval of the pastor? not a parish-based group?

◆ *New members.* Will we let new members join us once we have begun the six weeks of discussions?

Agree on housekeeping.

◆ *When will we meet?*

◆ *How often will we meet?* Meeting weekly or every other week is best if you can manage it. William Riley remarks, "Meetings once a month are too distant from each other for the threads of the last session not to be lost" *(The Bible Study Group: An Owner's Manual).*

◆ *How long will meetings run?*

◆ *Where will we meet?*

◆ *Is any setup needed?* Christine Dodd writes that "the problem with meeting in a place like a church hall is that it can be very soul-destroying" given the cold, impersonal feel of many church facilities. If you have to meet in a church facility, Dodd recommends doing something to make the area homey *(Making Scripture Work).*

◆ *Who will host the meetings?* Leaders and hosts are not necessarily the same people.

◆ *Will we have refreshments?* Who will provide them? Don Cousins and Judson Poling make this recommendation: "Serve refreshments if you like, but save snacks and other foods for the end of the meeting to minimize distractions" *(Leader's Guide 1).*

◆ *What about child care?* Most experienced leaders of Bible discussion groups discourage bringing infants or other children to adult Bible discussions.

Agree on leadership. You need someone to facilitate—to keep the discussion on track, to see that everyone has a chance to speak, to help the group stay on schedule. Rena Duff, editor of the newsletter *Sharing God's Word Today,* recommends having two or three people take turns leading the discussions.

It's okay if the leader is not an expert on the Bible. You have this booklet, and if questions come up that no one can answer, you can delegate a participant to do a little research between meetings. Perhaps someone on the pastoral staff of your parish could offer advice. Or help may be available from your diocesan catechetical office or a local Catholic institution of higher learning.

It's important for the leader to set an example of listening, to draw out the quieter members (and occasionally restrain the more vocal ones), to move the group on when it gets stuck, to remind the members of their agreements, and to summarize what the group is accomplishing.

Bible discussion is an opportunity to experience the fulfillment of Jesus' promise "Where two or three are gathered in my name, I am there among them" (Matthew 18:20). Put your discussion group in Jesus' hands. Pray for the guidance of the Spirit. And have a great time exploring God's word together!

Y ou can use this booklet just as well for individual study as for group discussion. While discussing the Bible with other people can be a rich experience, there are advantages to reading on your own. For example:

◆ You can focus on the points that interest you most.

◆ You can go at your own pace.

◆ You can be completely relaxed and unashamedly honest in your answers to all the questions, since you don't have to share them with anyone!

Our suggestions for using this booklet on your own are these:

◆ Don't skip the Questions to Begin. The questions can help you as an individual reader warm up to the topic of the reading.

◆ Take your time on the Questions for Careful Reading and the Questions for Application. While a group will probably not have enough time to work on all the questions, you can allow yourself the time to consider all of them if you are using the booklet by yourself.

◆ After reading the Guide to the Reading, go back and reread the Scripture text before doing the Questions for Application.

◆ Take the time to look up all the parenthetical Scripture references.

◆ Since you control the pace, give yourself plenty of opportunities to reflect on the meaning of Matthew's account of Jesus' passion. Let your reading be an opportunity for these words to become God's words to you.

Bibles

The following editions of the Bible contain the full set of biblical books recognized by the Catholic Church, along with a great deal of useful explanatory material:
- ◆ The Catholic Study Bible (Oxford University Press), which uses the text of the New American Bible
- ◆ The Catholic Bible: Personal Study Edition (Oxford University Press), which also uses the text of the New American Bible
- ◆ The New Jerusalem Bible, the regular (not the reader's) edition (Doubleday)

Books

- ◆ Raymond Edward Brown, *The Death of the Messiah* (New York: Doubleday, 1994).
- ◆ J. C. Fenton, *The Matthew Passion* (Minneapolis, Minn.: Augsburg, 1996).
- ◆ Daniel J. Harrington, *The Gospel of Matthew* (Collegeville, Minn.: Liturgical Press, 1991).
- ◆ John P. Meier, *Matthew* (Wilmington, Del.: M. Glazier, 1980).
- ◆ Richard John Neuhaus, *Death on a Friday Afternoon* (New York: Basic Books, 2000).

How has Scripture had an impact on your life? Was this booklet helpful to you in your study of the Bible? Please send comments, suggestions, and personal experiences to Kevin Perrotta, General Editor, Trade Editorial Department, Loyola Press, 3441 N. Ashland Ave., Chicago, IL 60657.